A+ books

TRANSPORTATION IN MY COMMUNITY

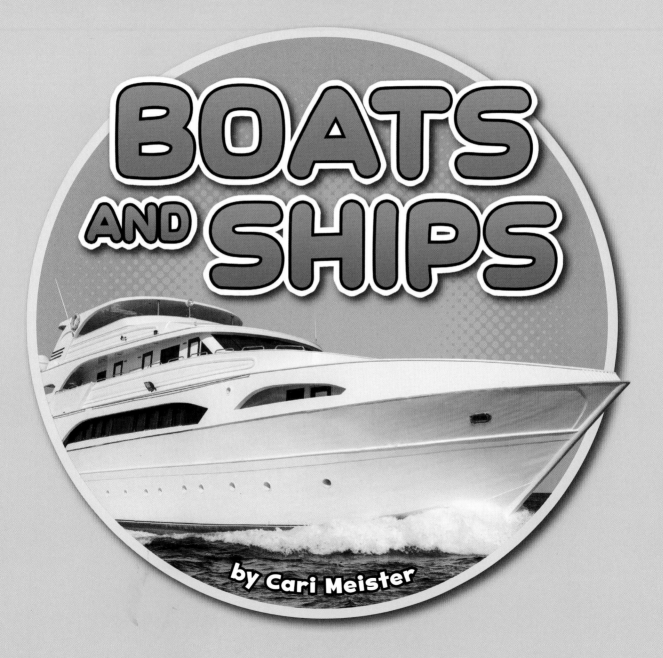

BOATS AND SHIPS

by Cari Meister

PEBBLE
a capstone imprint

Put on a life jacket.
Climb aboard.
Let's go for a boat ride.

ZOOOOM!

Boats float in the water.

hull →

The bottom is called the hull.

bow

The front of the boat is the bow.

stern

The back is the stern.

There are many kinds of boats.
Ferries take people and cars
across the water.

Tugboats push and pull big ships.

SPLISH!

SPLASH!

Canoes and kayaks are small boats.
They carry one to two people inside.
Riders paddle to get these boats moving.

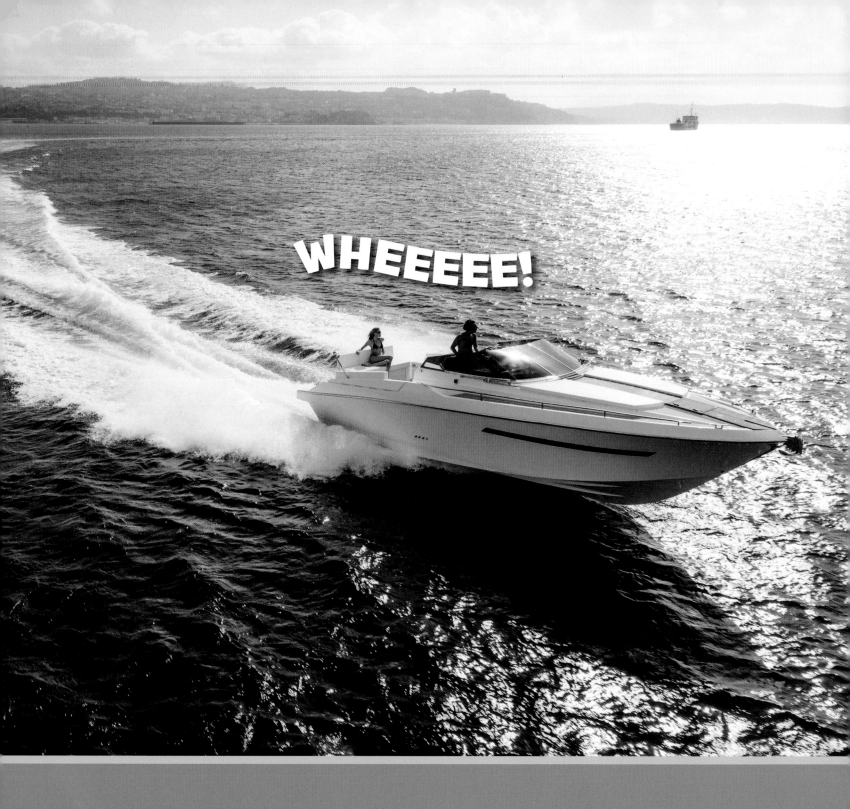

WHEEEEE!

There goes a speedboat.
It races through the water.

People use these boats for fun.
You can go waterskiing.

A cabin cruiser approaches.

The cabin cruiser's hull is shaped like a big V.
It smoothly cuts through the waves.

Look at the sailboats racing!
The wind catches the sails.
It pushes the boats through the water.

WHOOOOOSH!

Yachts are big, fancy boats.
People can use them to explore
the world.

Yachts have kitchens,
bathrooms, and bedrooms.
Some even have hot tubs.

Ships are big boats.
Icebreaker ships cut through icebergs.
Tanker ships carry oil and other fuel.

All aboard!

People take vacations on cruise ships.
These big ships may have pools, restaurants,
and movie theaters on board.

They sail to beautiful places.
Some cruise ships can carry
up to 5,000 people.

Cargo ships haul goods instead of passengers. They travel across seas and oceans.

A reefer ship is a refrigerated cargo ship.
It carries fruit, meats, and other food.

Military ships help keep us safe.
They watch over our land and seas.

They help people in need.
Battleships carry missiles and cannons.

BLUB. BLUB. BLUB.

Submarines move slowly underwater.
U.S. Navy submarines protect aircraft carriers.
They can launch missiles and torpedoes in the water.

Scientists use submarines to observe sea animals.
Submarines help people discover new things.

Engineers are always thinking of new boats.
They work to make boats faster and more powerful.

What kind of boat would you like to see next?

Timeline

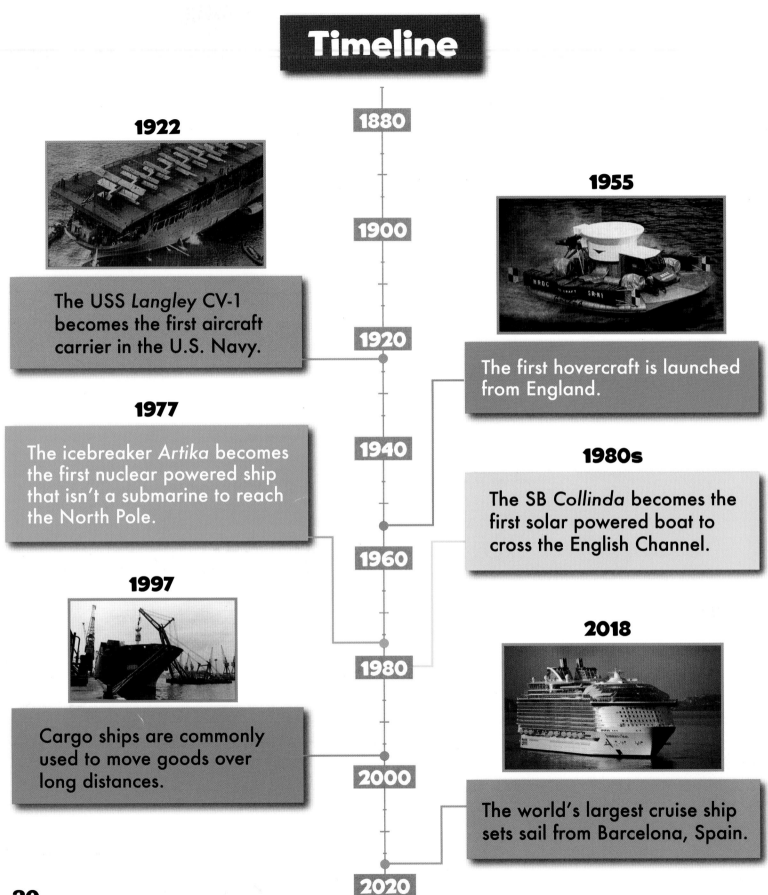

1922
The USS *Langley* CV-1 becomes the first aircraft carrier in the U.S. Navy.

1955
The first hovercraft is launched from England.

1977
The icebreaker *Artika* becomes the first nuclear powered ship that isn't a submarine to reach the North Pole.

1980s
The SB *Collinda* becomes the first solar powered boat to cross the English Channel.

1997
Cargo ships are commonly used to move goods over long distances.

2018
The world's largest cruise ship sets sail from Barcelona, Spain.

1880
1900
1920
1940
1960
1980
2000
2020

Glossary

aircraft carrier (AIR-kraft KA-ree-ur)—a warship with a large, flat deck where aircraft take off and land

engineer (en-juh-NEER)—a person trained to design and build machines

hovercraft (HUHV-ur-kraft)—a vehicle that travels on a cushion of air

iceberg (EYESS-berg)—a huge piece of ice that floats in the ocean

life jacket (LIFE JAK-it)—a device that keeps you afloat in the water

passenger (PASS-uhn-jur)—someone other than the driver who rides in a vehicle such as a boat or ship

torpedo (tor-PEE-doh)—an underwater weapon that explodes when it hits a target

Read More

Aloian, Sam. *How a Ship Is Built.* Engineering Our World. New York: Gareth Stevens Publishing, 2016.

Stark, William N. *Mighty Military Ships.* Military Machines on Duty. North Mankato, Minn.: Capstone Press, 2016.

Vamos, Samantha R. *Alphabet Boats.* Watertown, Mass.: Charlesbridge, 2018.

Internet Sites

Use FactHound to find Internet sites related to this book.

Visit www.facthound.com
Just type in 9781977102508 and go.

Super-cool stuff! Check out projects, games and lots more at **www.capstonekids.com**

Index

A+ Books are published by Pebble,
1710 Roe Crest Drive, North Mankato, Minnesota 56003
www.mycapstone.com

Library of Congress Cataloging-in-Publication Data
Library of Congress Cataloging-in-Publication data is available on the Library of Congress website.
ISBN: 978-1-9771-0250-8 (library binding)
ISBN: 978-1-9771-0502-8 (paperback)
ISBN: 978-1-9771-0254-6 (eBook PDF)

Editorial Credits
Michelle Parkin, editor; Rachel Tesch, designer; Heather Mauldin, media researcher; Katy LaVigne, production specialist

Photo Credits
Alamy: Trinity Mirror/Mirrorpix, 30 (bottom left); Getty Images: Topical Press Agency/Stringer, 30 (top left), Universal History Archive, 30 (top right), Wild Horizon, 27; iStockphoto: AndyL, 24-25, BergmannD, 25 (inset), kentarus, 16-17, pidjoe, 7, spooh, 29, von Brandis, 4-5; Shutterstock: Alan Budman, 12, aragami12345s, 15, Dan Logan, 23, Dan Thornberg, cover (bottom middle), Darren Baker, 5 (inset bottom), EvrenKalinbacak, 22, Federico Rostagno, cover (bottom left), Flamingo Images, 28, FOTOGRIN, 26, freevideophotoagency, 5 (inset top), 10, GERARD BOTTINO, 30 (bottom right), Kanok Sulaiman, cover (bottom right), Macgork, 13, MKeerati, 18-19, Paul Vinten, cover (top), 1, Philip Bird LRPS CPAGB, 11, Rawpixel.com, 20-21, richardjohnson, 6, trek6500, 8-9, Yari Ghidone, 14, Yevgen Belich, 2-3

Printed and bound in the United States of America.
PA49